# STRATHENDRICK

## *In Old Photographs*

A Selection from Drymen and District
Local History Society's Collection

*By*

Mary B. Bruce
and
Alison Brown

Stirling District Libraries
**1990**

# *Acknowledgements*

This publication would not have been possible without the interest and support of many local residents who gave their time and valuable information. Our thanks are also due to the following who generously loaned or gave photographs or gave assistance or advice in other ways:

Mrs H. Aitken, Mr G. Brown, Mrs Hannah Brown, Mrs Isabella Brown, Mrs A. Cameron, Mr A. A. Campbell, Mrs D. Duncanson, Mrs A. Gibb, Mrs J. Goodwin, Mrs G. Johnstone, Mr and Mrs H. McArthur, Mr O. McDonald, Mrs M. McKechnie, Mr J. McQueen, Mr A. Mitchell, Mr J. Rae, Mr S. Shearlaw, Mr T. R. Simpson, Mrs H. Smith, Miss I. Taylor, Miss N. M. Toland, Mr and Mrs G. Turner, and also MAC Images, Glasgow for help with the map.

Drymen and District Local History Society acknowledges with thanks the financial support of Stirling District Arts Council towards the establishment of its photographic collection.

Gifts of old photographs of the people and scenes of this area are always most welcome. Please contact Alison Brown, Community Librarian, Drymen Library, The Square, Drymen, G63 0BL. Telephone (0360) 60751.

**A Note of Caution!**

Readers who may find their interest aroused in some of the old buildings featured in this book should be reminded that they are all on private ground and should only be visited with the owner's consent.

ISBN 1 870542 16 9

Printed by
Cordfall Limited
Tel: 041 332 4640

**Craigton House, Fintry.** In the first half of the 19th century the Dun family bought farms in Fintry from the Duke of Montrose. In 1860 a son, William who was a senior partner in the Outram Press replaced the farmhouse at Craigton, one mile east of Culcreuch and above the Gonachan, with this large Victorian mansion house. He never lived in it but stayed with his sister at Bridgend. Later it was occupied by a nephew and a nephew's son, both named J. C. Waters. The latter changed his name to Dunwaters. In 1919 it was bought by Mr Rottenberg also of the Outram Press. He used it only in summer and as a result it deteriorated until it was finally demolished in the early 1940s. The Duns also farmed the Lurg, Bridgend and Spittalhill for many generations. They are buried in a mausoleum at Craigton.

**Burnside Cottage, Fintry.** Mrs Catherine Strang, second from right, outside her home at the end of the last century. She was the maternal grandmother of the late Mrs Margaret Gardner (née McDougall).

**Mrs Strang at her spinning wheel.** Again at Burnside Cottage and busily occupied amongst the equipment used in the spinning of wool. She was a well-kent person and known to all as "Granny Strang". On the stool on the left lie a pair of wool cards (flat boards with sharp metal teeth to tease the wool fibres straight). On the right is the winder for turning the yarn from the spinning wheel into hanks.

**Mr Archibald Strang, Fintry.** Mr Strang was the husband of Granny Strang and was beadle and grave-digger at Fintry Parish Church. This photograph is dated 4th February, 1904.

**Wedding Day in Fintry.** Bethia Hunter with pony and trap on her wedding day. The tallest man is "Big" Jardine, who farmed Kilunan and also had a fruit farm at Croftinstilly. Mrs Strang sits on the extreme left outside Fintry Inn. On the right of the close is the Toll House (home of Mrs Adams) and the Post Office. A story is told of a well-known cattle-dealer called Corrachoile, last century. His herdsmen were on their way to the Falkirk Tryst with their large herds of cattle. "Corrie" rode forward and offered the toll-keeper £5 for a free toll for one hour. The toll-keeper readily lifted the toll-bar. It can be imagined how great the droves were when the toll-keeper reckoned he had lost £10 in the deal. The toll for cattle was one old penny per head so about 3,600 passed through the toll in one hour.

**Street Scene in Fintry.** Mr William Edmond, general merchant, carter and coal merchant and tenant of Kilunan Farm is walking with the Rev. William McKean Campbell, parish minister at Fintry from 1896-1904. Mrs Edmond at the shop door bends down to speak to Margaret Ramsay. Mr Strang is back left, facing Mr Bob Duncan (with walking stick). The flags are out to celebrate the arrival of Sir Walter Menzies who had bought Culcreuch Estate. He was M.P. for South Lanarkshire, and in 1907 he built the Menzies Hall and gave it to the village to mark the coming of age of his son, James.

**Part of the old Cotton Mill, Fintry.** A large cotton factory was built about 1796 by Mr Peter Speirs of Culcreuch. Newtown, the present village was built to house the workers, the houses being on one side of the road and the gardens on the opposite side sloping down to the Endrick. The Cotton Mill originally had a fourth storey which was gutted by fire and not replaced when the building was re-roofed. In 1841 the mill was employing 260 workers. There was also a small woollen mill and a distillery. By 1850 all three had ceased to function largely due to the cost of transporting coal, cotton and yarn and also due to steam taking the place of water power. The mill is owned by Mr and Mrs M. Seymour.

**Mains of Glinns.** This laird's house, three miles from Fintry on the old Kippen road, was built for Moses Buchanan, second son of John Buchanan of Carbeth. Over the doorway the inscription MB MC 1743 is carved on the lintel. In 1970 when this photograph was taken it was roofless and a ruin. One of the last persons to live there was an aunt of Robert Dougall, the newscaster who as a boy used to holiday there. In the mid 1970s it was restored to an attractive two-storeyed house of considerable architectural interest. It is owned at present by Mr and Mrs L. Irvine.

**Main Street, Fintry, looking east.** The house on the right is Rose Cottage, the home of the Wilson family since the early 1900s. The Wilsons were well known in Strathendrick firstly as builders then as carriers serving the district for many years, and the firm is still active and based in Fintry. The photograph shows their first lorry parked at the gate.

**Mr James Rae selling milk about 1950.** Although every household had milk delivered, milk bottles and milk cartons were unknown in country districts. Mr Rae used a measure to fill the ladies' milk jugs from a 10 gallon milk can fitted at the back of his Austin car. The front passenger seat had been removed to accommodate a second 10 gallon can of milk. Mrs Hermiston is in the centre and on the right is her daughter Jenny (now of Larbert).

**Harvesting at Kilunan Farm, Fintry.** In a more relaxed age, Clydesdale horses enjoy a brief halt while Mr Rae and a worker make an adjustment to the binder, under the watchful eye of his collie. Mr Rae farmed Kilunan from 1940-1971.

**Cornfield, Kilunan Farm.** A sight, almost forgotten, of stooks set up to dry in the wind and all placed at the same angle to the sun to ripen.

**Harvesting at the Mains Farm, Balfron about 1960.** This Massey-Ferguson combine-harvester was one of the first privately owned in the Balfron area. Mr Alex Pirie is at the steering wheel and Mr Hugh Sanderson is behind. Mr Pirie came to the Mains about 1933 and his son James and grandsons Sandy and Jim farm there now.

**Ballindalloch Cotton Mill, Balfron 1789-1898.** Mr Robert Dunmore of Ballikinrain and other businessmen introduced cotton-spinning to Balfron when a large mill was built in 1789 near to the present bowling green. For many years hand-loom weaving prospered with at one time 400 looms working. As steam power, dependant on coal, took the place of water-power there was a succession of owners and the industry declined. Latterly H. W. Pollock & Co. set up a shirt factory in it and employed about 40 women. In 1893 the empty building was purchased by Mr Archibald E. Orr-Ewing of Ballikinrain and later demolished. Balfron was the first village in Scotland to be lit by coal-gas, a by-product of the mill. This year Balfron celebrated the bicentenary of Ballindalloch Mill and by timely coincidence the village has piped gas this year as it linked up to British Gas.

16

**Ballindalloch Hotel, Balfron.** At the south end of Buchanan Street stood Ballindalloch Hotel, next to the Mill House and across the road from what is now Shearer's Garage. It was a popular tourist, commercial and family hotel. It was an excellent base for touring, fishing and golf as Balfron had its own 9-hole course at Tombrake (visitors 1/- per day). As with most hotels in the district posting was an important service. Carriages, landaus, brakes, waggonettes and pony-carts were available for guests and parties arriving at or departing from the station. At the end of last century the hotel was owned by Mr John Malcolm. Mr Johnny Fraser (father of Mr Alex Fraser) was head groom. It was later taken over by Mr Robert Dunkeld, the man in the bowler hat, whose name appears above the door.

**Balfron Parish Church at the end of last century.** The original church from the mid-seventeenth century was in a dubious state of repair being dependant on the generosity of its heritors. It was rebuilt in 1832 by John Herbertson of Glasgow with a square tower above the entrance. An oblong building, it had galleries along three sides. Some fifty years later considerable changes were made with the main door being placed at the north end, the pulpit at the south and transepts being added. The trees in the middle of the photograph are gone but the old Clachan Oak on the left still stands, encircled with three iron bands to which the "jougs" (iron collars) were attached to punish offenders. A granite fountain now stands in front. It was erected in 1892 at the north end of Buchanan Street where the bank is, to the memory of Dr William McCandlish, but was later resited at the Church. The war memorial has since been erected nearby.

18

**Cotton Street, Balfron about 1916.** Originally named Virgin Row, it was renamed Cotton Street when workers from Ballindalloch Cotton Mill occupied the houses there. Balfron School is on the left of the large tree. The white buildings on the right go back to 1760 and were the property of Mr and Mrs David McKinnon, the small building on the east end being a sweet shop, well patronised by the school children. All were demolished in 1981 and Hillview was built on the site, now the home of Mrs Jean Shearer and family.

**The Tontine Hotel, Balfron, about 1900.** The dark building at the north end of Buchanan Street was the "Tontine". The white building on its right was "Rockbrae", home of Mrs J. Venables who was in charge for many years of the shirt factory down the street. Mr James Gray held a licence for the hotel but when Balfron went "dry" it became a temperance hotel. At this time the other licensed premises were the Ballindalloch Hotel and the Endrick Public Bar owned by the Gilroy family and situated at the corner of Dunmore Street and Buchanan Street.

**Awaiting passengers at the Tontine Hotel.** This photograph, taken in the 1920s, shows Rankin Bros. Bus Service which was taken over by Wm Alexander & Sons of Falkirk in 1929. The bus was an American ambulance from the First World War. The driver was Mr Alex. Young and on the right Mr John Brown, father of Jock, Jim and Danny.

**Balfron Higher Grade School Group, 1935, Class 3A.**
Back Row: J. Blair, A. Mathieson, J. Hamilton, A. Dowie, W. Williamson, T. Ferguson, C. Wilson, I. McNicol, W. Alexander.
3rd Row: A McLaren, J. Goodwin, R. Cairns, J. Sinclair, J. Ullstrom, D. Forrest, J. McKellar, A. Fisher, J. Denovan, D. Anderson, D. Anderson.
2nd Row: Mr Robertson, M. Dowie, J. King, McDonald, McColl, M. Kaye, M. Black, M. Wood, I. Kirkland, M. MacIntosh, J. Wilson, Miss Coutts.
Front Row: E. Rattray, J. Sinclair, M. Dun, P. Herd, E. Bilsland, J. Gordon, M. McAllister, N. Retson, x. *Note x = unidentified.*

**Miss Lawless' Dancing Class, Balfron, 1947.**
Back Row: Miss Rena Lawless, J. Ferrie, N. Steel, A. Blaikie,
M. McVicar, F. McKinlay, M. Stewart, W. Forsyth, A. Speight,
M. McArthur, J. Harper, J. McArthur, x.

Front Row: x, H. McLellan, M. McAllister, J. McAllister,
I. Cunningham, I. Gilroy, M. Landels.
The class practised in the Waverley Hall, Balfron.
*Note x = unidentified.*

**Shortbread Mould and Wedding Cake Banners.**

**Mr William Lockhart, Master Baker, Balfron.** The Lockhart family were well-known bakers in Strathendrick, Mr Wm. Lockhart starting his bakery in 1860. Vans made deliveries daily to Aberfoyle, Gartmore, Buchlyvie, Killearn and Fintry. Their shortbread was famous, being dispatched in tins all over the world. They made wedding cakes for all the large weddings in the area. There was a break of a few years before his son Malcolm took over the business in 1922 which the Lockhart family carried on until 1936. Mrs Helen Smith is a grand-daughter and Mr J. Edgar Lockhart a grandson of Mr Wm. Lockhart.

**The Smiddy, Dunmore Street, Balfron.** On the right is Mr John Taylor, master blacksmith, with his assistant, Mr John McIntyre, Wester Thirds, Gartmore. This photograph was taken over seventy years ago. Mrs Taylor and her baby son have come along for the special occasion of the photographer's visit. Miss Isa Taylor is a daughter of Mr and Mrs Taylor.

**Buchanan Street, Balfron, looking to the Campsies.** After cotton-spinning had ceased at Ballindalloch Mill part of the building was used as a shirt factory, made possible by the development of the sewing-machine. Finishing was done in homes owning sewing-machines. The first used in Balfron was a Wheeler and Wilson machine between 1860 and 1870. In 1896 A. B. Grant & Co. opened a branch factory in premises previously owned by the late Mr Andrew Graham and seen behind the child on the left of the photograph. The factory gave employment to about 30 women. In 1920 the old mill sewing-machines were scrapped and new machines powered by an oil engine installed.

**Balfron Road, Killearn.** On the left of the telegraph pole is the old red sandstone toll house which operated up to 1878. On the wall of the house is a list of the toll rates in 1841, e.g. a cow – one old penny, a horse and cart – six pence ($2\frac{1}{2}$p in today's currency). On the right is the White Horse Inn owned in the early 1900s by Mrs Bruce, grandmother of Mr Frank Bruce. It was demolished in the 1940s and the ground is now the Health Centre car park.

**At Blairessan, Killearn.** Blairessan House was built in 1899 by Sir David Wilson for his mother. The Simpsons did the joinery work and when it was completed the joiners' bill for the house (with very fine yellow pine panelling), the stables and the lodge was £1,080. Eight generations of the Simpson family ran the joiners' business in Killearn from 1735 to 1981. In this photograph are:
Standing: Bob Simpson, Archie Simpson and an employee.
Seated: An employee and Robert Simpson (Rennie's grandfather who died in 1905).

**Mrs James Simpson, Killearn.** A very attractive picture of Miss Catherine Mowbray Rennie who came to Killearn last century. She married and was the mother of Robert, Rennie and James. Her husband was an outstanding athlete, well-known as a hurdler and runner.

**The Black Bull Hotel, Killearn.** This photograph was taken before the 1914-1918 War. On the left is Mrs D. L. Bennie, mother of Mr Johnstone Bennie, Drymen. Her mother, Mrs Blair and her son are with her at the hotel entrance. The building had been extended from the original inn which was on the main drove road through Fintry to the Falkirk Tryst. Lack of custom forced the Bennies to give up the Hotel at the start of the War. The stables and farm-steading were on the right of the building.

**The Square, Killearn.** In the centre is the 103 feet high monument erected in 1788 in memory of George Buchanan (1506-1582). He was a brilliant scholar, linguist, mathematician and satirist, and for three years was tutor to the young James VI. He was born in the old farmhouse at the Moss on the River Blane. On the right are the original 18th century houses, purchased and renovated by the Killearn Trust in the mid 1930s. On the left is Cameron's Cabin, long since demolished. Cameron lived alone but he had a few close drinking pals. One night after having had too much to drink they had a disagreement and Cameron had them charged with breaking in and attempted murder.

**Killearn School Group, about 1919.** Just within living memory. Mr James Shearer was headmaster for 26 years retiring in 1935. Those identified are:

2nd Row: 2nd J. Paul (Mrs D. McGeachie), 3rd A. McGowan, 5th J. McGregor (Mrs P. Clark), 8th M. Orr (Mrs W. Knights).

3rd Row: 5th G. Gibson, 6th Robert Simpson, 8th Rennie Simpson.

Back Row: 2nd J. Davidson, 7th I. Sinclair.

**Killearn Primary School, about 1936.**
Back Row: A. Ferrier, x, x, W. McMillan, W. Stevenson, x, J. Brown, A. King, J. McGowan, D. McKinnon.
3rd Row: E. McKeich, J. Fallas, H. Allan, F. Ponton, J. McMartin, R. Baird, M. McKay, I. Blane, M. Crawford, M. Simpson.
2nd Row: M. Bruce, A. Bruce, N. McMillan, W. Campbell, J. McNeill, E. Hutcheson, J. McEwan, A. Campbell, S. McKinlay, C. McKinlay
Front Row: S. Robertson, A. Clelland, J. Fallas, B. Loudon, J. Moir, G. Dingley, S. Winters.
*Note:x = unidentified.*

**Main Street, Killearn.** The shop at the corner of the two-storey building was Mrs Campbell's "sweetie" shop. She made up "jeelie pieces" (bread and jam) for the school children at playtime. Her husband was a painter and in the winter months when work was quiet he made "teuch jeans' (chewy candy). Note the water tap on the gable end of the shop.

**Football Team, Killearn about 1900.** The five footballers in the photograph were known as the "Hellish Five". Back Row: Hugh Watson (trainer), Matthew McKellar (uncle of Duncan), Bob Simpson, Sandy Munro (trainer). Front Row: James Simpson (Rennie's father), Bob Munro, John MacGregor (blacksmith). Bob was an exceptionally good player and had a chance to play for Celtic.

**Killearn Sports Day, 11th June 1938.**
The members of the sports committee and officials are:
Standing: T. Paul, P. Ferguson (headmaster), A. MacDonald, J. Strain, D. Johnston, J. McGowan, A. Clelland, A. Bilsland, D. Clelland, W. McMillan, J. Brown (Westerton). In front: G. Muir, H. Watson, A. Gilfillan, J. Brown (Spittal).

**Killearn Miniature Rifle Club, 1930s.** The club was formed in the early 1900s and met in a hut near to the old Killearn railway station. Due to lack of support it was disbanded after the Second World War.
Standing at the back: A. Law, R. Sinclair, A. Paterson, I. MacBoyle, W. McGowan Sen., D. Paterson, Mr MacBoyle, Johnnie Brown, J. Clinton.
Middle Row: B. King, J. Sinclair, W. Clinton, J. McGowan, W. Hill, C. MacBoyle, James Brown.
Seated: B. Paul, Sir Norman Orr-Ewing (Captain) H. Muir.
The two large trophies are the Fanshawe and the Connell cups.

**The Blane Smiddy, 1950s.** For many years this blacksmith's was known as Wilson's Smiddy, called after the owner. He was followed by Mr D. McNeill who ran the smithy from 1928 to 1944. Mr Duncan Sinclair, his nephew, trained under him and took over the business on his uncle's death. It is now a precision engineering business run by Mr Michael Cowie who took it over in 1983 and did extensive alterations to the building.

**The Bilsland Family, late 1890s.** Mr Walter Bilsland farmed Little Drumquharn through which the Endrick winds before passing under Killearn Bridge. This attractive picture strongly reflects the personalities of the sitters.
Standing: Peter (who later farmed Meikle Drumquharn). Agnes (later Mrs McNeill, Blane Smiddy and mother of Mrs J. Goodwin and Mrs A. Gibb) and Jeanie (who died at Blane Smiddy in 1987 in her 102nd year and was known as "Auntie Jeanie").
Seated: Mrs Bilsland, son Walter who was accidentally drowned in the Pot of Gartness aged 30 years, and Mr Walter Bilsland.

**Croy Cunningham.** The farmhouse stands high above the River Blane where it meets the Endrick. It goes back a long time in history, having been associated with the Earls of Lennox. Through inheritance, purchase, marriage or division the land passed from Cunninghams to Buchanans and by 1763 was owned by the Duke of Montrose. In 1834 James, 3rd Duke of Montrose sold it to Mr Peter Blackburn of Killearn. The farmhouse was renovated extensively at the end of the 1940s by the late Mr George Campbell. The present owner is his nephew, Mr A. A. Campbell.

**Killearn Hospital, 1941-1972.** In 1938 the Secretary of State for Scotland commissioned Killearn Hospital to be built as an emergency military hospital. It was completed in 1941. After the war the hospital comprised of 404 beds, orthopaedic, neurosurgical and medical. In 1948 on the nationalisation of the health service Killearn Hospital came under the board of Management for Glasgow Western Hospitals. In 1972 the Neurosurgical Unit moved to the Southern General Hospital. It was internationally famous and the largest unit of its kind in the world at that time. The Orthopaedic and Medical Units moved to Gartnavel General Hospital and the buildings at Killearn Hospital fell into disuse. They are at present being demolished and there are plans for an equestrian centre.

**Killearn House.** The original Place of Killearn was built in 1688 and was the seat of a branch of the Grahams of Montrose. About 1812 the house and estate were purchased by Mr John Blackburn, a Glasgow sugar merchant, and the above house was built at Croy Leckie, now part of Killearn Home Farm. Killearn House remained in the Blackburn family until it was inherited with the estate by Curtis Lampson, a son of the heiress Helen Blackburn who married Norman Lampson in 1874. Mr David Young Sen., of Killearn Home Farm purchased the mansion house in 1961 from Mr D. McPhail who had owned it for 21 years. It is now derelict.

**Finnich School Group, about 1913.**
Back Row: Miss Proctor, A. Morton, J. Walker, R. Orr, John King, W. McNicol, J. Stewart, W. Stewart.
Middle Row: J. McLaren, E. Begg, I. King (Mrs I. Brown), J. Young, Jean King, J. McNicol, F. Begg, A. Orr, C. Wilson.
Front Row: D. McLaren. K. McLaren, (Mrs K. Brown), A. King, J. Orr, T. Miller, Dan McLaren, S. Brown, J. Young.

As many as fifty pupils attended this two-roomed school but after the opening of Croftamie School in 1907 the numbers at Finnich School declined until it closed down in 1924. There was a toll house opposite the school.

**The King Family, Finnich Malise Lodge, 1915.**
Back Row: James, Margaret, Tom and John.
Front Row: Isabella (Mrs Brown, Balfron), Mr Robert King, David (Royal Engineers), Allan and Mrs King (née Jessie Bell). Mr King was coachman for fifty years to Mr John Wilson of Finnich Malise, a Glasgow shipowner. The original lodge was on the right side of the gate. As the King family grew, the house was far too small and the present lodge in the background of the picture was built opposite and the original demolished.

**The McGregors of Catterbog, 1909.** The McGregor family have been associated with Strathendrick for a very long time. They lived at Drymen Bridge before leasing Catterbog in 1874. They were well-known as carriers, mainly of wood. As they were willing to accept work anywhere their business took them far afield. They had stabling for six horses at Catterbog, but used three times that number when needed.

R. McGregor (cousin), Dan MacGregor (uncle of the present Dan), P. Gibb, J. McMartin, Duncan McGregor (late husband of Mrs E. McGregor), Andrew McGregor (father of the present Andrew).

45

**The Ruins of Mains Castle, Kilmaronock.** From the middle of the 15th century the Cunninghams, Earls of Glencairn, owned extensive lands in the parishes of Kilmaronock and Balfron. In the latter, they owned forests and Ballindalloch. All that remains of a large, imposing stronghold is the ruined tower with walls that were nine feet thick. James, 14th Earl of Glencairn (1749-1791) was a friend of Robert Burns.

**Kilmaronock Church about 1900.** Built in 1813 on the site of the old church of St. Marnock. Two gravestones in the churchyard date back to the 17th century. On the right of the church doorway is the upper section of a grey sandstone slab with very unusual markings. It is known locally as "The Crusader's Stone". In a wood nearby is the spring known as St Marnock's or St Ronan's well, famous in earlier times for the curative properties of the water.

**The Goldie Family, Kilmaronock Manse.** The Rev. W. McL. Goldie B.D. and Mrs Goldie, with William (later Dr Wm. N. M. Goldie) and Winifred (Mrs Bilsland). Mr Goldie was Minister of Kilmaronock Parish Church from 1902 -1948 and Mrs G. Turner's maternal grandfather.

**At the Wards Farm, Gartocharn about 1920s**. Mr Tommy Mackay, postman. The wheel in the background pumped water from the low-lying flooded ground into a channel which returned it to the River Endrick. The wheel is no longer there.

**Presentation to Mr T. B. Shearer**. Under the paraffin lamp in the Village Hall, Mr Shearer, organist and choirmaster at Kilmaronock Parish Church for 26 years, is presented by Miss Mitchell with an electric reading lamp.

Back Row: x, Miss M. Mitchell, G. Turner, Miss Mellis, Miss A. Martin, Miss J. Graham, Miss B. Forshaw, Miss S. Wyllie, J. MacFarlane, J. Mitchell, Miss L. Taylor, Miss K. Lang, D. Lawson.

Middle Row: Miss Shearer, Mrs T. Shearer, Miss M. Mitchell, Mr T. B. Shearer, Mrs Goldie, Rev. W. McL. Goldie.

Seated: Miss M. Gray, Mrs Lang.

*Note: x= unidentified*

**Girls' Club Dance, Old Schoolhouse, Gartocharn.**
Lady Leith-Buchanan started the Girls' Club at the end of the last war.
Seated are Miss K. Mitchell, Miss A. McMaster, J. Friar, Miss A. Porter, Miss N. Davidson, M. Hannan, M. Hutchison N. McMaster.
Others in the picture are P. Fraser, Miss F. Fraser, Miss M. Smith, P. Davidson, P. Mitchell.

**Tug of War Team, Drymen Games, 1890s.** The games were held annually in the Show Field, Drymen Bridge. They go back a long time and ceased at the outbreak of the Second World War.

Those identified in the picture are in the front row: 2nd A. Orr (Coldrach Farm), 3rd W. Orr (Overballoch, Balloch), 4th Walter Bilsland (Badshalloch, paternal grandfather of Mrs G. Turner).

**Drymen Games in the 1930s.** Aberfoyle and Gartmore Games and Drymen Games had many competitors and supporters in common. Officials from the one organisation acted as judges and umpires for the other.

The important guests at this Games are Mr J. Anderson (Dundee), Mr W. P. Maclay, an official, Mr J. Morrison (Glasgow, an ex-heavyweight champion of Scotland), Mr A. Ferguson (Dundee), and Mr A. Doughty of Renagour, Chieftain of the Aberfoyle and Gartmore Highland Games.

**Drymen Show Committee and Judges, 1952.** Strathendrick Agricultural Society have held a show in the Show Field at Drymen Bridge annually since 1816 except during war years and on two occasions when the Show had to be cancelled due to exceptional rainfall. This photograph shows:

Back Row: A. Renfrew, W. Hosie, P. Clark, H. Allan, A. Davidson, O. McDonald, A. McAdam, W. Burton (Judge of B.-F. Sheep), x, W. Allan, D. McIntosh (Judge of Clydesdales), x, W. Orr, G. McDonald, J. McQueen Jnr., and unidentified Judge of Friesians.

Front Row: A. Jessiman, S. McKechnie Sen., R. Hay, J. McQueen Sen., J. M. Bannerman (later Lord Bannerman), D. Middlemass, J. Allan, A. Lyon (Judge of Ayrshires) J. Barr (Judge of Ayrshires).

*Notes: x = unidentified.*

***Pride of Endrick*, Reg. No. MS3273.** A record of the day when a threshing contractor came with his steam traction engine and threshing machine to a Strathendrick farm. This traction engine was built in 1920 for Strathendrick Farmers. The 12-ton machine was typical of the heavy steam engine used in the fields, on the roads and in industry before the combustion engine. *Pride of Endrick* was owned by Raines of Stirling between 1921 and 1945 and then by Sharp Brothers of Forres. It was later sold to an English showman who restored it in 1962, added a canopy roof with the multi-coloured electric lamps of the fairground. This photograph was kindly supplied by Mr R. A. R. Smith of Glasgow Museum of Transport (at the Kelvin Hall) where *Pride of Endrick* may now be viewed.

**Strathendrick Bowlers.** When this photograph was taken Balfron was the only village with a bowling green. In 1936 a green was laid at the Buchanan Arms Hotel and Drymen Bowling Club was formed.

Back Row: T. McGlone, J. Alston, D. Thomson, D. McCluckie, J. Taylor, J. Toland, D. T. Morton.
Front Row: R. Caldwell, G. Buchanan, A. Lochhead, B. McKinlay, D. McNeill, J. Walker.

**Strathendrick Golf Club Outing to Buchanan Castle, early 1920s.** The Course and Club House of Strathendrick Golf Club were opened on 5th October, 1901 by Lady Helen Graham. Each year the Duke of Montrose entertained members and their friends at Buchanan Castle. Among the guests are:

Front Row: W. Scott, Dr J. MacKinnon, R. A. Murray, J. Wilson (Finnich Malise), J. W. Murray, The Duke of Montrose (President), D. McCluckie, Rev. S. Ewing, A. B. Simpson, W.W. Murray. 2nd row: N. Davidson, G.O. McGregor (Duke's Trainer and vet), D.Wilkie, W. McGregor, Miss P. Simpson, Miss M. Wilkie, Rev. J. T. Monteith, J. Sinclair, W. Kirk, Miss A. Aitken, Miss J. Renfrew, Mrs W. McGregor, J. Howe, A. Murray.

3rd Row: B. Buchanan, x, Mrs Dunlop, J. D. Dunlop, A. Hosie, J. MacKinnon, W. Lockhart, J. Hall, D. McCallum, J. Aitken, G. Mitchell.

4th Row: J. Buchanan, G. Buchanan, J. McGregor, J. Veitch, T. Kerr, C. Murray,.

Back Row: J. Marshall, Miss M. MacKinnon, Miss I. Bilsland, Rev. W. Lacey, Lady Helen Graham, Mrs Murray, Miss Mitchell, Miss M. Scott, J. E. Stuart, H. Graham.

*Note: x= unidentified.*

**A Sunday Morning at Ballat Farm.** Mr and Mrs James McDonald of Ballat ready to leave with their son George for his christening at Gartmore Parish Church. The trap is drawn by Polly. Mrs McDonald was born at Ballat Farm and lived her whole life there.

**Oliver McDonald** and his nanny, Miss Jean MacDiarmid, Ballat Farm, 1911.

**The Funeral of Mr James McDonald of Ballat, 1919**. As the coffin is carried throught the gates of the Gartmore Churchyard this moving scene is recorded for posterity. After three hundred years of McDonalds farming at Ballat, Mr and Mrs Oliver McDonald gave up the farm in 1987 and retired to Drymen. His family had been the longest continuing tenants of the Duke of Montrose having farmed Boreland and Gartfarran before purchasing Ballat.

**Buchanan Castle in the 1920s.** Designed by William Burn, Buchanan Castle was built in grey sandstone for the 4th Duke of Montrose between 1854 and 1855 to replace Buchanan Old House, destroyed by fire in 1852. The castle contained over 40 bedrooms, several large public rooms and a kitchen wing on the extreme right of the picture. On the top of the left-hand turret stood "The Watchman", a life-sized Highlander blowing a trumpet and holding a pike. When James, 5th Duke of Montrose died in 1925 the death duties were enormous and in due course it became evident that the family could not maintain the castle. The farmhouse at Auchmar was extended in 1932 and it became the family home.

Buchanan Castle, Drymen

**Buchanan Castle from the South-East**. Around 1936 the castle was used as a guest house. From 1938 it served as a military hospital. In May 1941 Rudolf Hess was taken there for a few days to be treated for slight injuries sustained when landing by Messerschmidt at Dungavel, near Glasgow. After the war various organisations considered purchasing the building but nothing materialised. The interior was stripped and the roof removed in 1955. Angus Graham, the 7th Duke was for many years Minister of Agriculture for Rhodesia. He now lives in Scotland. His eldest son, the Marquis of Graham farms at Auchmar, Drymen.

**Montrose House, Balmaha.** Built in 1891 by the Duchess of Montrose to give a "fresh-air fortnight" to Glasgow children who would otherwise not have had a holiday. It was built with stone costing 4 shillings (20p) per ton from the red sandstone quarry on the bank of the Catter Burn at Croftamie.

**The Liquor Works of Turnbull & Co., Balmaha.** The picture shows Balmaha Cottage, the chemical works with the chimney stack, the bothy, stable and byre and Bay Cottage. In summer all the stocks of coppice trees from the lochside were brought in and stacked up in the yards. At the end of last century about 700 tons of small wood were used annually in the manufacture of pyroligneous acid and its by-products. When the synthetic manufacture of Turkey-red dye was introduced the acid was no longer required, the works became superfluous and the chimney stack was demolished about 1923 after having been in use for over 100 years.